THE DEADLIEST DINOSAURS

BY **'DINO' DON LESSEM**

ILLUSTRATIONS BY **JOHN BINDON**

LERNER BOOKS • LONDON • NEW YORK • MINNEAPOLIS

To Hall Train, one of the least nasty and most talented of all dinosaur people

At present, only a few fossils exist of *Megaraptor*, *Pyroraptor* and *Variraptor*. In depicting these dinosaurs, the artist drew from the fossil evidence and from what is known of the appearance of other similar dinosaurs.

First published in the United Kingdom in 2009 by
Lerner Books,
Dalton House,
60 Windsor Avenue,
London SW19 2RR

Website address: www.lernerbooks.co.uk

This edition was updated and edited for UK publication by Discovery Books Ltd.,
First Floor, 2 College Street, Ludlow, Shropshire SY8 1AN

Words in **bold type** are explained in the glossary on page 32.

British Library Cataloguing in Publication Data

Lessem, Don
  The deadliest dinosaurs. - 2nd ed. - (Meet the dinosaurs)
  1. Dinosaurs - Behavior - Juvenile literature 2. Dinosaurs
  - Defenses - Juvenile literature 3. Dinosaurs - Juvenile
  literature
  I. Title
  567.9'12

ISBN-13: 978 0 7613 4340 0

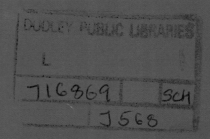
Printed in Singapore

TABLE OF CONTENTS

MEET THE DEADLIEST DINOSAURS

WELCOME, DINOSAUR FANS!

I'm 'Dino' Don. I LOVE dinosaurs. I even love deadly dinosaurs. Raptors were the scariest, deadliest dinosaurs of all. I'm just glad we were not alive when they were! Come and see them here. It's safe to look.

DEINONYCHUS
Length: 3.5 metres
Home: western North America
Time: 115 million years ago

DROMAEOSAURUS
Length: 2 metres
Home: western North America
Time: 76 million years ago

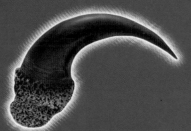

MEGARAPTOR
Length: 8 metres
Home: South America
Time: 86 million years ago
Only parts of its leg and giant arm claw have been found.

MICRORAPTOR
Length: 50 centimetres
Home: Asia
Time: 124 million years ago

PYRORAPTOR
Length: 1.7 metres
Home: western Europe
Time: 69 million years ago

UTAHRAPTOR
Length: 6 metres
Home: western North America
Time: 125 million years ago

VARIRAPTOR
Length: 2.5 metres
Home: western Europe
Time: 71 million years ago

VELOCIRAPTOR
Length: 2 metres
Home: Asia
Time: 80 million years ago

VERY DEADLY DINOSAURS

One of the deadliest of all dinosaurs is hunting. Its name is *Utahraptor*. It's almost as big as an ice cream van. It has huge claws and sharp teeth. Running quickly, *Utahraptor* chases after a huge plant-eating dinosaur.

The plant eater is nearly as long as a tennis court. That's longer than three *Utahraptor*. It probably weighs as much as 10 of them. However, the plant eater is helpless against the claws and teeth of this very deadly dinosaur.

THE TIME OF THE DEADLIEST DINOSAURS

Utahraptor

Deinonychus

125 million
years ago

115 million
years ago

Utahraptor and its relatives are the most deadly dinosaurs known. Some people call them **raptor dinosaurs.** Raptor dinosaurs lived 125 million to 65 million years ago. Most of them were small meat eaters. Like other meat eaters, raptors had sharp teeth for killing.

Velociraptor

Dromaeosaurus

Pyroraptor

80 million
years ago

76 million
years ago

69 million
years ago

However, these deadly dinosaurs were
different from other meat-eating dinosaurs.
Raptor dinosaurs had big curved claws. They
used their claws to slice their **prey,** the
animals they hunted and ate. Raptors had
long, rod-like tails. These may have helped
them balance while they chased their prey.

DINOSAUR FOSSIL FINDS

The numbers on the map on page 11 show some of the places where people have found fossils of the dinosaurs in this book. You can match each number on the map to the name and picture of the dinosaurs on this page.

1. Deinonychus   2. Dromaeosaurus   3. Megaraptor   4. Microraptor

5. Pyroraptor   6. Utahraptor   7. Variraptor   8. Velociraptor

Raptors and other dinosaurs died out many millions of years ago. All that we know about them comes from **fossils.** Fossils are traces left by animals and plants that have died. Scientists have found fossils of raptor dinosaur bones, teeth and claws, mostly on the northern continents.

Fossils help scientists to understand what raptor dinosaurs looked like and how they lived. Fossils of claws and jaws also help scientists to work out which dinosaurs were the deadliest. The deadliest dinosaurs had killer claws and powerful jaws.

Fossils show us that some raptor dinosaurs were tiny, as small as puppies. Others were as long as two cars. None of them were even half the size of a big meat eater like *Tyrannosaurus rex.* Why were some raptor dinosaurs so small?

Scientists think they had a special job in nature. Small raptors such as *Pyroraptor* probably hunted lizards, small animals and other little dinosaurs. Raptors that ate such small prey couldn't grow very large.

Size doesn't matter when it comes to nastiness. Raptors were deadly hunters, no matter how big they were. By teaming up, small raptors could take on animals that were much bigger than themselves.

Some raptor dinosaurs were even deadly to each other. A fossil of a baby *Velociraptor* was found with tooth marks in its head. Another *Velociraptor* might have killed it!

KILLER CLAWS AND JAWS

We are in the desert in the eastern part of central Asia, 80 million years ago. A *Velociraptor* is attacking a *Protoceratops*. Suddenly, the sand dune that they are fighting on caves in. The dinosaurs are both buried in the sand.

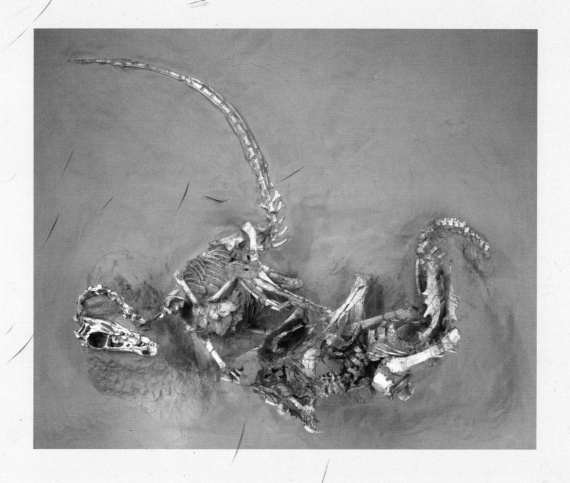

Researchers found the fossils of these two dinosaurs in 1971. Their **skeletons** were nearly complete. The dinosaurs were found in the same position that they were in when they died. Their fossils showed scientists how raptors used their claws and jaws.

The claws on a raptor's hands and feet
were its biggest weapon. Raptor claws
were curved and sharp to hook onto prey.
Raptors had one giant claw on each limb.
They could pull the claw back, just like a
cat pulls back its claws. That way, raptors
could run without dragging their claws.

When a raptor caught up with its prey, it jumped and swiped. It slashed with its hands and feet. Its claws sliced open its victim. No dinosaur had deadlier weapons.

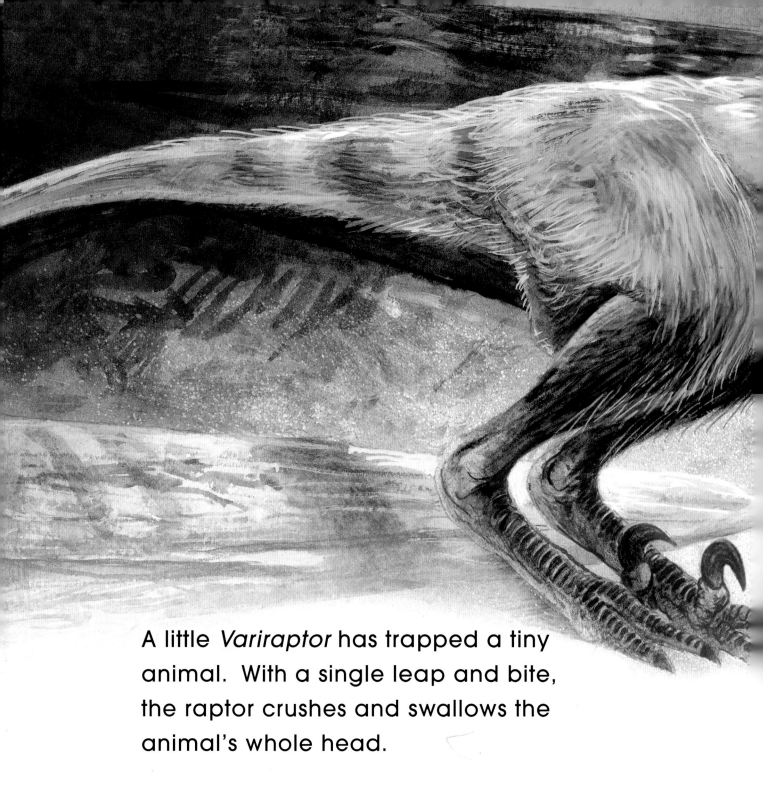

A little *Variraptor* has trapped a tiny animal. With a single leap and bite, the raptor crushes and swallows the animal's whole head.

Variraptor had small, narrow jaws filled with pointed teeth. Each tooth had grooves like those on a steak knife for sawing through meat. *Variraptor* could tear even a larger animal in two.

Raptors, such as these human-sized
Deinonychus, might have hunted in
groups called **packs.** This pack has
come across an injured *Gastonia,* a
large armoured dinosaur.

Deinonychus is quick enough to dart in
and around the dying dinosaur. Several
Deinonychus use their claws to attack the
armoured dinosaur. They slash at its soft
belly with their huge, sharp claws. Together,
the raptors will easily finish off their prey.

RAPTOR DISCOVERIES

The first raptor ever discovered was
Dromaeosaurus. Its fossils were found in
western Canada in 1914. *Dromaeosaurus*
was no bigger than a golden retriever dog,
but it had a much longer tail.

Dromaeosaurus was a clever hunter. Its teeth were sharp, with ridges for slicing meat. Other raptors had the same type of teeth. *Dromaeosaurus* had an unusually wide, strong head for its size.

In 2000, the discovery of *Microraptor* fossils in China excited scientists all over the world. *Microraptor* is one of the smallest dinosaurs ever found. It was no bigger than a crow.

Microraptor was closely related to birds. It was a nasty dinosaur with sharp claws. We don't know for certain what it ate. Perhaps it hunted lizards, tiny animals, insects or even birds!

Scientist Jim Kirkland found a fossil of the largest kind of raptor in 1991. Dr Kirkland's team dug up the claw of a *Utahraptor*.

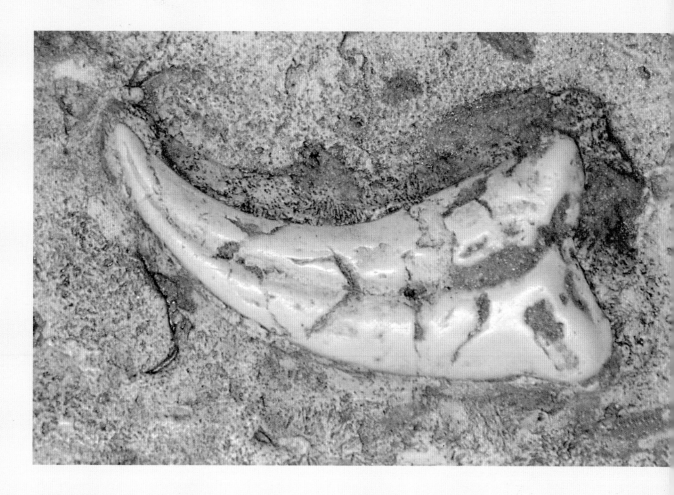

Utahraptor was a fast and deadly hunter.
Its toe claw was razor sharp and longer
than your foot. *Utahraptor* also had sharp
teeth, good eyes and strong legs. Perhaps
Utahraptor was the deadliest dinosaur of
them all.

Imagine a killer dinosaur as long as a bus, with claws twice as long as a banana! Such a frightening creature lived in South America 86 million years ago. Its name was *Megaraptor*. It could have hunted huge prey like this *Rebbachisaurus*.

Most of what we know about *Megaraptor* comes from one fossilized leg and a huge claw. However, scientists hope to discover more. *Megaraptor* isn't closely related to true raptor dinosaurs, but it was still a deadly, giant-clawed dinosaur!

GLOSSARY

fossils: the remains, tracks or traces of something that lived long ago

packs: small groups of animals that live, eat and travel together

prey: animals that other animals hunt and eat

raptor dinosaurs: meat-eating dinosaurs with a claw on each foot and long, rod-like tails

skeleton: the framework of bones in the body

INDEX

Text copyright © 2005 by Dino Don, Inc.
Illustrations copyright © 2005 by John Bindon
First published in the United States of America in 2005.
Photographs courtesy of: © Denis Finnin, American Museum of Natural History, p 17; © Francois Gohier, p 28; © Ron Timblin, Dino Don, Inc., p 29.